This book is a game changer! *After reading these skills, I believe this book could be an exit class for every college senior. The conversational tone, coupled with compelling stories draws the reader in and makes the book relatable. My student athletes at Lewis and Clark University will be required to read this book.*

—**Marcus Lattimore**, Former Collegiate & NFL Running Back, Assistant Football Coach & Life Coach at Lewis and Clark University, blogger, MarcusLattimore.com

What a timely contribution! *This practical, easy-to-read guide is sure to enhance the life of anyone who reads it. While intended for those beginning the journey of adulting, everyone is likely to find a new skill to challenge their status quo. Each chapter pairs solid, real-world guidance with questions sure to inspire further thought, and the suggestions take all the guesswork out of how to put these ideas into practice. The included resources are recent and relevant, allowing for further learning and exploration when ready. The authors' down-to-earth writing style and practical examples are sure to appeal to all audiences. This book delivers in a most marvelous way!*

—**Sarah E. Wright**, Psy.D., Certified Sex Therapist and Licensed Psychologist, author of *Redefining Trauma: Understanding and Coping with a Cortisoaked Brain*

Praise for *Launch: A Guide to Adulting*

Messy and Marvelous perfectly encapsulates the chaos and confusion I experienced while breaking into the adult world. Although I was acting as the perfect source of strength and insight on how to navigate that world, I did not know what I was doing! It is a necessary read for anyone unwilling to settle for less than they can be!

—**Emily Deahl**, Singer/Songwriter, Nashville, TN, @emilydeahl

I wish I'd read **Launch: A Guide to Adulting** *forty-five years ago, as I was preparing to enroll in college. The book has invaluable advice about what it means to live responsibly in an adult world; or better, how to live as a responsible adult in the real world. The wisdom Amy Sander Montanez and Rhea Ann Merck share with their readers is both practical and necessary. Especially helpful is that they offer ways to practice those skills—from asking for help when we most need it to developing personal "grit"—by doing such simple things as thinking reflectively about our lives, journaling, practicing good health habits, and developing financial acumen. While I wish I'd read the book more than four decades ago, I'm glad I've read it now, and know that I will read it several times over, trusting that it is helping me to navigate the treacherous waters of what is ultimately a messy (and yes, marvelous) life.*

—**Mark Sibley-Jones**, Ph.D., Author of *By The Red Glare*, English Teacher at the South Carolina Governor's School for the Arts, Adjunct Professor at University of South Carolina, Upstate

WISDOM FOR NAVIGATING YOUR
MESSY MARVELOUS LIFE

Launch

A Guide to Adulting

AMY SANDER MONTANEZ

RHEA ANN MERCK

Managing Editor
Robbin Brent

Cover and Interior Design
Andrew Breitenberg

Compositor
Rick Soldin

Marketing, Social Media, and General 21st Century Advisement
Maria Montanez

Readers and General Suggestions
Emily Deahl, Leigh Poteat, Maria Montanez, Mark Sibley-Jones, Marcus and Miranda Lattimore, Sarah E. Wright

Publishing Consultant
Jeffery Schwalk

MessyMarvelous Logo Design
Helen Johnson Creatives

Administrative Assistance
Karen Garrison

Library of Congress Control Number: 2020921166

ISBN Printed edition: 978-1-7357870-0-8
ISBN Digital edition: 978-1-7357870-1-5

Printed in the United States of America.

To all of the young people in whom we rest our hope and our future.

May this book be a guide for you as you navigate this Messy Marvelous world.

We believe in you.

Contents

Acknowledgments

First and foremost, we are eternally grateful to the loyal readers of our blog. Along the way we have received so much encouragement, validation, and suggestions for stepping out onto a bigger stage. Many of you told us to write a book, so here is our first book!

This book would not have been possible, truly, without the thoughtful guidance of Robbin Brent, who, upon first reading, completely understood our goal and expressed her belief in us and this work. She has been generous beyond measure, with her time, energy, expertise, and enthusiasm for our writing. Robbin, you are a jewel.

We want to thank our young adult clients, students, friends, and daughters, who keep us in the loop of the world they are navigating, and help us understand what is needed to find not only success but happiness along the way.

On a more personal note

from Amy

I count my husband, Nick, and my daughter, Maria, as foundational to my well-being and perspective on the world. Their love, humor, willing hearts, challenging natures, and encouragement in all I undertake make so much about this messy life more marvelous. They are my joy, and I am eternally grateful. I am one of the lucky ones.

My friend, colleague, co-writer, and go-to human, Rhea Merck, has graced my life for over 25 years. I think we have covered every topic, personal and collective, and to be known and loved so deeply is grace upon grace. She fills my dry well often and I am forever grateful. To my wide community of beloved friends, I trust you know how much I love you.

My Christian faith informs all of what I write, even when I am not mentioning it explicitly. It is a daily touchstone for me, and I write from a place of continuously integrating the truths of psychology and spirituality. The God I believe in is a God of love. As the Presiding Bishop of The Episcopal Church, Michael Curry has said, *"If it isn't about love, it isn't about God."* I wrestle with the practical realities of this belief often, as love is not always easy.

from Rhea

I am eternally grateful for the love, warmth, and humor I experience in my relationships with my daughters, Caitlin and Rebekah. They have been my teachers in so many ways and continually inform my worldview. I would not be the person I am today had they not graced my life. I am also grateful to my partner, Alberto, who supports my dreams and aspirations and who lovingly cooks and cares for me when I am trying to keep up with my messy life. I could not do this business of writing without all of the clients and students who are willing to share their journeys with me.

Finally, I am grateful to my vast network of friends who are always supportive and who fill in all the gaps with laughter and fun along this journey of life. These deeply intimate friendships are my richest gifts in this world. This especially includes Amy, without whom Messy Marvelous would not be possible. Our shared dreams of what this is, and can evolve into, gives our work its fire and direction. Amy gracefully embodies the ideal true friend: she has picked me up when my life has fallen apart and celebrates generously when we turn each of life's corners together. It is always a gamble to go into business with a friend but I believe our success lies in our communication skills, our deep love for one another, and the unwillingness to sacrifice our friendship for a business.

INTRODUCTION to the Messy Marvelous Guide to Adulting

The creative use of the noun "adult" as a verb seems to go back to a 2008 tweet:

> *Grew up in a town of 2k and adulted 10 years in NYC.*
> *Same values. Keeping the job.*
> *Feeding the family. Educating the kids. Buying the stuff.*
> —unholytwerp@unholytwerp

By 2016, the verb became a highly used noun again, but this time as the word "adulting." That same year, *Time Magazine's* June 8th issue ran a story about the increased use of the word, citing that the American Dialect Society nominated the verb "adult" as the year's most creative construction. Its meaning was "to behave in an adult manner, to engage in activities associated with adulthood." Merriam-Webster confirmed that the word exploded in 2016. As a verb, to "adult" is to behave like an adult, specifically to do the things—often mundane—that an adult is expected to do. And as a gerund or noun, "adulting is hard to do."

So this book is for you if you are between the ages of 18 and 35. Or maybe even older if you still need help adulting/launching. This book is for you if you are in college, have graduated, or maybe never made it all the way through. It's also for you if you decided college wasn't for you and you are already earning your way through life. This book is for you if you are male, female, gay, straight, queer, trans, or any other identity. This book is for you if you are single, married, partnered, monogamous, or not. This book is for you if you live in the North, South, East, West, or Middle America. It may even be for you if you live in another country. It's for you if you live in a rural, urban, or suburban setting. This book is for you whether you are religious or not, and also no matter what your religion is.

How can a book be so inclusive? Why are we bold enough to think our audience is this broad? Because the skills necessary for adulting are mostly universal. We all need to learn a few skills in order to function well in adult life, whether that be in our families, our partnerships, our careers, our communities, or our nation.

You may already know that this book started as a blog which you can find at messymarvelous.com. We started the blog because many of our friends, students, and clients told us that they needed skills to navigate life. As the blog took shape, we realized that our blogs could be categorized, often by themes, and that our readers were asking for skills in certain areas. One of those areas was "adulting." The skills are universal, meaning they can help you in all areas of your life. This book need not be read front to back. Dive into any section that seems relevant to you and enjoy.

We have included a few reflection and discussion questions after each skill. You can think about these on your own, of course; or you could use this as an opportunity to connect with others (Skill # 6: Find Your People) and get a few friends together and see what they think. Several of our test readers suggested having a monthly get-together, book-club style, as an opportunity to talk about one skill at a time, do some connecting, and learn from each other. Some of the questions could even be used at work for staff meeting discussions. Be creative.

We have also included a checklist of actionable items if you're not sure how to take these ideas and make them go live. These are concrete ways to incorporate the skills into your life. The checklist includes a journal cue as Skill #1 suggests that you start a journal. Many people drop journaling after a few days because they lose interest in daily ramblings. There are many ways to journal and tackling a specific topic for a deep dive is an alternative. Finally, there is a list of resources: TedTalks, podcasts, movies, and books. We would love to hear from you if you have any other great sources for us to add.

Let us know how you are using the skills. Also let us know if other skills come to mind that would be helpful with your adulting.

Life is messy and marvelous, dear Readers. Good luck with your adulting!

Amy & Rhea

"Don't be afraid to ask questions. Don't be afraid to ask for help when you need it. I do that every day. Asking for help isn't a sign of weakness, it's a sign of strength. It shows you have the courage to admit when you don't know something, and to learn something new."

—Barack Obama

Ask for Help

by *Amy*

Are you scratching your head? Why would a book on adulting start with a skill about asking for help? After all, aren't adults supposed to know what to do and solve their own problems? This feels quite counter-intuitive, doesn't it?

Several years ago, my daughter and a group of her early-twenties friends were gathered around my kitchen table. The topic of discussion that day was the most important quality in a future mate. I was listening carefully, my back to them as I stirred a pot of chili, pondering their list: kind, truthful, helpful, good work ethic, willing to communicate, God-centered, good to their parents, sexual attraction—I cannot remember the others. At some point one of the girls asked me directly, "Mama Montanez, what do you think is the most important quality in a mate?"

"The willingness to ask for help when it is needed," I responded. Silence. "Why do you think that is the MOST important quality?" another girl asked.

I can tell you. It is because **LIFE IS MESSY** and sometimes we just don't know enough or have enough resources or have the strength to do it well on our own. Sometimes life hands out more than we think we can bear. Sometimes we have blind spots and can't see our own problems. Having been a therapist for thirty years now, and a teacher before that, my perception is that the most successful and well-adjusted people know when to ask for help. The people I know who are making a real difference in the world ask for help.

There is research showing that asking for help is easier for women than for men. Perhaps some women do value collaboration more than some men. Perhaps women are more willing to be influenced by others, as John and Julie Gottman discovered in their longitudinal research into successful relationships. But I actually think this skill is difficult for everyone trying to make it in the adult world. What will my colleagues think of me if I ask for help? Will that make me too vulnerable to office gossip and put me on the bottom of the professional food chain? How do I ask for help understanding and managing my finances in this dizzying, virtual world? My parents expect me to launch and I still feel the need to be tethered. And what about my relationships? I can't seem to figure those out either. Help!

In real life, in this messy, crazy life we are living, it is impossible to know everything. As an example, accountants and financial planners exist because we all do not have the skills or the knowledge to do a good job maximizing and managing our finances. There is too much information to know and we may not even have the inclination or desire to learn. So, if we didn't ask for help in this area, it is very possible that our finances wouldn't be managed as well as they could. Finances can become a wreck very quickly, making life even messier.

Some of us hire mechanics to fix our cars because we don't have the skills or the knowledge to do it, and we don't have the desire nor the time to figure it out ourselves. So we ask for help. Volumes of people ask for help from personal trainers and nutritionists without giving it a second thought.

Asking friends for help is certainly an adulting skill. Help me think about this. Help me see my blind spots. Help me find some compassion. Help me, Friend, in whatever ways I do not seem to be able to help myself.

A wise man can learn more from a foolish question than a fool can learn from a wise answer. —Bruce Lee

Barbara Coloroso, a parenting consultant and international speaker, encourages parents to give their kids this message: "There is no problem so big or so complicated that you and I together cannot figure it out. AND IF WE CAN'T, we will find someone who can help us!" What an affirming and positive message, and a life strategy that promotes resilience. Help is available and we will get it when needed.

I have heard emerging adults tell me that they live with fear of asking a question to which they don't already know the answer. To my ears, this sounds like crazy-speak, but I have heard it so often that I know it is a part of the current culture. In Brene' Brown's best-selling book, *Daring Greatly,* we get a glimpse into the why of this issue. "Eighty-five percent of the men and women we interviewed for shame research could recall a school incident from their childhood that was so shaming, it changed the way they thought of themselves as learners." (p. 189). As children, we spend most of our daytime hours in school. If we are shamed in any way, told that we aren't good enough at writing, math, comprehension, music—anything—then shame takes hold. And shame, according to Brown, breeds fear. And when we are afraid, we do not ask courageous questions.

Founder and CEO of Spanx, Sarah Blakely, offers this advice as an anti-dote: *"Don't be intimidated by what you don't know. That can be your greatest strength and ensure that you do things differently from everyone else."* Write that one down on an index card and tape it somewhere you can see it every day!

For some reason, asking for help from a therapist or coach feels threatening to many. We are not only saying we need help, but we know we may have to admit how and when we are wrong, and that might feel shameful and embarrassing. And so things get messier and messier until there is a true threat, like the relationship might be over, or the job is in jeopardy, and then it seems like maybe asking for help is a last-ditch effort. "Better sooner than later" is a good mantra for adulting.

Life is hard and life is messy. Many of us don't have all of the personal, interpersonal, and life skills necessary to fully support a successful launch into adulthood. Perhaps we didn't have good role models in our homes. We had childhood trauma that affected and continues to affect our development. Maybe we are afraid of communication. We don't know how to speak our truths. We have buried our pain with addictive behavior and by building walls. Possibly we are still immature and selfish. We cannot admit our faults and negative patterns and we are defensive, blaming others for our own problems. Life has handed us something completely overwhelming and we are unprepared to deal with it constructively. Probably the list is endless. But the truth is that asking for help and getting good help can change the messy into marvelous. And if you are getting help, and the messy isn't changing, get different and better help. Things can and do change. We need skills, support, and accountability to make changes. We need others who know more than we do and can guide us on the journey.

Adulting is messy and marvelous. So learn to ask for help.

LAUNCH Questions for Reflection and Discussion

What messages have you gotten in your life about asking for help? For example, were you told to figure things out for yourself? Were you ever shamed or belittled when you asked for help? What messages did you get about cooperation and collaboration?

What experiences have you had when you have asked for help? If an experience has been positive, what made it so?

What places in your life are you least likely to ask for help? Why? What makes these areas off limits?

Right now, in the moment, is there an area of your life that needs help? Are you willing to ask? Why or why not?

Notes:

LAUNCH Checklist

☐ Start a journal. Throughout this book we will offer journal tips for each skill. For this skill, write about what stumbling blocks keep you from asking for help. Journal about what might help you break through those barriers and get the help you need.

☐ If you are looking for a therapist, you can always ask your primary care doctor or a friend. Also, www.psychologytoday.com is a wonderful resource that lists therapists in your area and their areas of expertise. There are also organizations, like www.betterhelp.com, www.talkspace.com that use apps and online therapy exclusively.

☐ Consider the activities that take up a lot of your time that you hate. Now, explore the possibility of paying someone else to do those things for you. Need someone to clean your house? Look at your budget and find a way to make that a priority. You get the idea.

☐ Practice making yourself vulnerable to a trusted friend or relative. Start slowly. Find someone who is a good listener and can help you think through the process. Ask for confidentiality. If it goes well and your issues are honored, you can go deeper.

LAUNCH Resources

Maybe You Should Talk To Someone, by Lori Gottlieb

All You Have To Do Is Ask: How To Master The Most Important Skill For Success, by Wayne Baker

Tedtalk: www.tedtalk.com *Asking For Help, Not A Weakness*, by Michele Sullivan

Tedtalk: www.TEDxsarasota.com *Real Men Ask For Help*, by Michael Hrostoski

If you could kick the person in the pants responsible for most of your trouble, you wouldn't sit for a month.

—Teddy Roosevelt

You hypocrite, first take the log out of your own eye, and then you will see clearly to take the speck out of your neighbor's eye.

—Jesus, Matthew 7:5 (NRSV)

Take Personal Responsibility

by *Amy*

Well, this doesn't sound like much fun, does it? Adulting just got really hard! You are responsible for your life. For your choices. For your feelings. For your reaction to things. For your thoughts. Your decisions. Your actions. Yeah, I kind of hate this sometimes, too, because I can be my own worst enemy. I make decisions that don't serve me or anyone else. Still, that is on me—still my responsibility.

Before you get defensive, I already know that shit happens. I know that much of what happens in life is out of our control. You did or did not get the job. Your car broke down and you don't have the money to fix it. You just haven't been able to save. The government shut down and you are out of work again. Your partner broke up with you. You fell and broke your arm. You got sick. It's all true. It's all messy.

AND, you have a choice about how to respond to any and all of what life sends your way. You can choose to respond in ways that may seem easy but will ultimately sabotage you. Let me give you a few examples of **how you can avoid taking responsibility**. You can:

> **Blame others.** So easy, isn't it, to just say it is someone else's fault and the reason that you are where you are. Sometimes your predicament is due to someone else's wrong-doing. It actually IS another person's fault. AND, you are still responsible for

how you respond to that. There is always a choice about how to respond. If you are not sure how to respond in a positive way when something is "done to you", refer back to Skill #1 [Ask for Help] and ask someone to help you figure it out.

Play the victim. "Poor, pitiful me. Why do bad things always happen to me?" Maybe you know this person, the one who assumes the position of being a punching bag for the world. Lacking any personal agency, the victims view themselves as passive, allowing the world to act upon them. This is a position of complete abdication of personal responsibility. If you want to watch a compelling YouTube video on this, google "stuck on an escalator-take action." We've all been there!

Whine and Complain. I do like to whine sometimes, to a friend or colleague, just for a minute or two. You know, when things are hard and not going the way I want them to. Or when someone is hanging on my last nerve. But trust me, a habit of whining and complaining will use up immense amounts of your energy reserve and will keep you from being able to assess what you might do next, and figuring out if something can shift. A friend of mine was recently whining, again, about not having enough money. Fair enough. He's running his own business and it's not going well. But the whining is keeping him in a stuck place. I tried a gentle confrontation that went something like this. "Hey, you've been talking a lot about not having enough money. Are you ready to brainstorm about some ways out of this predicament? I'd be happy to do that with you." His response: (Seriously!) "Not tonight. I just want to complain." Fair enough. But not helpful for him.

Fail to come up with solutions to your own problems. Isn't it easy to sit and do nothing? To let the path of inaction become the default answer? If you don't find solutions to your own problems, your passivity will become the ultimate saboteur.

Perhaps you've heard this definition of insanity: doing the same thing over and over and expecting different results. I've been insane and I know you have, too.

There are, however, **multiple benefits to be gained by learning to take personal responsibility.** And, it's not all hard and serious. For instance, you can gain:

A sense of empowerment. I can honestly say when I am consciously aware of taking responsibility for my life, I feel stronger and freer. My friend Pete has a saying, "I wish I could but I don't want to." It makes me laugh and happy every time I hear or think about it. It is his way of not apologizing while taking personal responsibility for his response to requests. Just saying "I don't want to" is powerful. It is equally powerful to say a clear "YES." Another favorite quote: "If you never say "no," your "yes" means nothing." When I say a clear yes, I feel confident and strong. Even if it is a yes about something I did wrong. Yes, I did that. Yes, I missed that deadline. Yes, I forgot to lock the car. Yes, I didn't pay that bill. If I have to call a creditor, I find a kinder person on the other end of the line when I just say, "I missed the due date. Can you do anything to help me with this late charge?"

A feeling of authenticity and being known. When I take responsibility for my actions, I am more my true self. When I say to someone, "I am late because I was trying to do too much at the last minute and I underestimated my time," they now know something real about me. When I say, "I know I said I would do that, and I haven't, and here's the reason: I said yes when I should have said no and I am working on that. I didn't want to do what you asked me to do but I didn't have the courage to tell you that." Now I feel known a little. And now I may be able to be more responsible the next time that happens.

It's so much better than blaming and whining! I just have to throw in another quote right here. It's so perfect.

A willingness to accept responsibility for one's own life is the source from which self-respect springs.
—Joan Didion

A creative life. This is such good news. You get to create a life. Repeat after me: "I get to create a life." Say it out loud. Say it in front of your friends. Shout it out the window. Truly. You don't always get to choose the content life gives to you, but you get to choose the process—the "how to" of dealing with what you are handed. Viewed in this way, taking responsibility for your life can be a creative, life-giving act. Even when handed a difficulty, taking responsibility offers you an opportunity to make art out of your life.

And always remember, if you are having trouble with this skill, refer again back to skill #1: Ask for help. Therapy, coaching, a good friend, a good minister, meditation, prayer—any of these can help us learn to take personal responsibility.

Adulting is messy and marvelous, so take personal responsibility.

LAUNCH Questions for Reflection and Discussion

When you make a mistake, what is your initial response (Be honest!)?
What would help you move beyond justifying, defending, or blaming?

Do you know how to make a good apology? Are you willing to practice?
We have included an apology "cheat sheet" at the end of this chapter to
help you get started. This is a skill in and of itself. Practice!

What are some internal cues that you are being defensive? For example,
finding yourself blaming a situation or circumstance for your behavior.
How can you begin to move toward more "real time" consciousness and
stay out of the defensive/blaming mode?

Are you willing to become more curious about yourself? For example,
asking yourself the "why" question might be helpful. "Why did I act
this way? What is it that I am having a hard time looking at in myself?"
You can change what you can name. Give it a try.

Notes:

LAUNCH Checklist

☐ Journal Tip: focus specifically on behaviors you want to change. List the problems that have happened because of that behavior and focus on what was going on with you during that interaction.

☐ Use active listening techniques. Listen to another without offering a rebuttal or advice. Just reflect back what the other person is saying until you truly understand them. (You don't have to agree, just understand.) www.verywellmind.com features active listening skills.

☐ Learn this mental filter, first used by the Sufis: Is it true? Is it appropriate? Is it necessary? Is it kind? You can read about this at www.messymarvelous.com/skill-34-speak-your-truth/

☐ Here's an exercise that takes some courage: Record yourself complaining about all your problems in life. Just free associate and talk outloud about all the things that are bothering you. Next, go back and listen to your recording. How did you feel about yourself listening to your complaining? Make a note. Time to stop and actually do something? I hope so, for your sake!

LAUNCH Resources

▨ *Why Won't You Apologize: Healing Big Betrayals And Everyday Hurts*, by Harriett Lerner

▨ Harriett Lerner and Brené Brown May 6, 2020 podcast on "UnLocking Us": *I'm Sorry: How To Apologize And Why It Matters*

▨ *How Can I Forgive You?: The Courage To Forgive, The Freedom Not To*, by Janis Abrams Spring

▨ *The Gift of Being Yourself*, by David Brenner (specifically Christian)

▨ *The Road Back To You: An Enneagram Journey To Self-Discovery*, by Ian Morgan Crone and Suzanne Stabile (also Ian's podcast, *Typology*)

Recipe for A Good Apology

—adapted from Janis Abrams-Spring: *How Can I Forgive You?*

Take unilateral responsibility for the hurt you have caused.

"I understand what I've done (to you, to the team, to my co-workers, my boss)." There is no "but" or "if only" attached.

Make your apology personal.

"I care about YOU, I know I hurt YOU, and I know that—given your specific background, personality, history, etc.—this would hurt you in this particular way."

Make your apology specific.

"Here is the truth of what I have done." Not with broad brushstrokes, but with fine details. "I hurt you in these specific ways."

Make your apology deep and meaningful. It must matter to you.

"I get it. I see your pain and your point. I know that I have done something wrong and hurt you. I understand you may not be able to trust me again." Saying "I'm sorry" is so often not enough. What are you sorry for?

Offer no excuses or rationalizations.

The apology is clean and one-sided. Never, "If you would have done this, I wouldn't have done that." The message has to be one of personal responsibility for your behavior. "We agreed on this, and I broke our agreement. It is totally my fault."

If necessary, apologize over and over.

The hurt you caused will come back because life will trigger the wound again.

Offer possible solutions and ask questions.

Say, "I want to earn your forgiveness and trust. I am willing to keep an eye on myself so I don't repeat this behavior. I have these ideas about how to do that. Do you have any ideas that are important to you that might help me?"

Share "Aha" moments.

For example, "I use to think this, but now I know this." Or, "Yesterday I realized again how awful this must have been for you." Or, "Watching that movie made me realize how off base I've been."

Become aware, going forward, of how to rebuild the relationship.

You have learned a lot about your partner, colleague, boss, friend. You know what you need to do. Now do it.

Knowing yourself is the beginning of all wisdom.

–Aristotle

Know Yourself

by *Rhea*

There's no better way to begin taking personal responsibility than by getting to know yourself. As a teacher, it is the joyous icing on the cake to see former students transitioning into adult life. Like the backbone of a good movie or a great novel, character development is vital. We love those characters that are complex in their honesty. Simple, cookie-cutter people are uninteresting. One dimension does not hold our attention for very long.

The truth is that we are all complex in many ways. We might initially follow the path set for us by our parents' expectations but eventually, and hopefully, that unfolds more fully as we enter adulthood. The rules and roles set for us in childhood are intended to offer a foundation from which we can fly. That foundation includes our values, traditions, belief system, and more. We might migrate far or we might nest nearby, but either way, we need to understand our own instincts and desires.

Why do we believe certain things? Do we just blindly do as we've been taught? Do we question ourselves? Or do we take the time and effort required to closely examine those beliefs? Do we broaden our experiences to see what more of the world is like and how other people live? Are we willing to test what we've been taught? Do we leave the comfort of "home"? Do we chance being uncomfortable?

I hope so. ...

Find out who you are and do it on purpose. —Dolly Parton

He calls me *Merck!* and I call him *JZ!* (no, not that one), but if those were your real initials, wouldn't you want to be called "JZ"? Anyway, JZ had to learn this lesson almost immediately after graduation when his father became terminally ill and died a few months later. JZ had been taught to lead a conventional life in a small town. In fact, he was a first-generation college student—perhaps already aspiring for something different in his life. Very shortly after his father's death, his mother moved and suddenly, there was no home to which he could return after college. So he quit his job, got out of a dead-end relationship, packed up necessities and his dog, and struck out on his own.

It was a Parsifal journey.

One of my favorite, most relatable stories is recounted in its symbolism by Jungian analyst, Robert Johnson, in his book, *He: Understanding Masculine Psychology*. Despite its subtitle, it is important to note that all of us have a masculine side of ourselves just like we all have a creative, nurturing, feminine side. With apologies for this cursory summary, Parsifal was one of King Arthur's knights who, as an emerging adult, set out from the comfort of his parents' home in search of the Holy Grail.

Parsifal encounters the typical challenges, battles, maidens, nymphs, evil, and good that one finds in all the stories of the Hero's journey. In my recollection, the story takes a turn when he realizes that one of the things working against him is the cloak his mother wrapped around him before he set out, and he eventually leaves it behind. What is revealed in the end is that the grail is really the self. The whole Self. The spiritual core of one's being. It abandons the materialistic world and accommodates the pull of opposites—our good *and* our bad; our light *and* our dark. It is the Divine woven from hardship, decisions, solitude, crises, connection, loss, individuation, and redemption. Parsifal sheds the cloak, which was symbolic of his mother's teachings, in order to be successful in his search. We can all relate to this tale. It is about the journey of *becoming*. Parsifal becomes a whole adult.

When we fight or ignore those parts of ourselves that we don't like, we are more likely to be harsh with ourselves and with others. I'm not especially fond of the part of myself that some people might call "lazy." That said, I sometimes prefer to spend a day on the couch and put off despised tasks, like sorting mail. But the awareness of my real need for rest, or help with certain tasks, makes me more compassionate when I recognize those same needs in others. I judge them less and am more kind to myself. Self-loathing, as you might imagine, is really bad for us in every way.

I'm not saying that you must abandon all that you learned from your family. But the important task is to examine what is working and what is not. Accepting our whole self allows us to be our best Self. The one who reserves judgment. The one who connects better with others. The one who can practice forgiveness. The one who can ask for help. The one who is whole and healed. The one who more closely embodies the Divine.

The more you know yourself, the more you forgive yourself. —Confucius

While I was in Colorado visiting a friend, I caught up with JZ, who was in a Master's degree program out there. We watched our football team play on TV, had a beer, and talked about his journey since leaving college. His wisdom was already shining as he shared the following.

I see a lot of people graduate and then go live with their parents because they really have nothing figured out. Going back to your hometown or to live with your parents is too comfortable. Challenges are necessary to grow. In my opinion, the fact that you're on your own, struggling, and trying to figure out life is what is special about that time. It's a sensitive time. It's how you get to know WHO YOU REALLY ARE. I'm thankful for the challenges I've faced and I know there is a 0% chance of me living a boring life.

Sweet, sweet icing. This guy is a gem. And I've no doubt he's grown because of how he's gotten to know himself. I'm also confident he will bring his best self, his whole Self, along wherever he travels.

Adulting is messy and marvelous, and the journey is long, so get to know yourself.

LAUNCH Questions for Reflection and Discussion

At what times in life have you learned the most about yourself? Consider times of transition, crisis, discomfort, heart-break, and any other times that call for a big life change.

We often learn our lessons in the rear-view mirror; what can you see with 20/20 vision that was not apparent before?

From whom are you willing to hear things about yourself that are hard to hear, that could be positive or negative? How willing are you to honestly reflect on this feedback?

Notes:

LAUNCH Checklist

☐ Journal Tip: Ask a few of your friends to list what they see as your five greatest strengths and your five greatest weaknesses.

☐ Take the RHETI, (Russ Hudson Enneagram Typology Inventory), an Enneagram assessment found at www.enneagraminstittue.com, and begin an exploration of your Enneagram type.

☐ Take the StrengthFinders 2.0 assessment, found at www.gallup.com/strengthsfinders

LAUNCH Resources

Gifts Differing: Understanding Personality Type, by Isabel Briggs Myers

The Wisdom of the Enneagram, by Don Richard Riso and Russ Hudson

Becoming Conscious, by Joseph Howell

Podcast: *The Real Enneagram* (Institute for Conscious Living)

*Everything is related to everything else, dammit Ms. Sander, and don't you **ever** forget it!*

—Dr. Charles Brewer, Furman University, Experimental Psychology class

Develop Personal Grit

by *Amy*

You might already be figuring this out as you are reading, but so many of these skills are intricately related. So much so that once you get better at one of the skills, you will also become better at the others. For instance, if you get better at taking personal responsibility, and you get better at asking for help, and you get better at knowing yourself, you are likely to be more able to develop personal grit and perseverance. Adulting well in one area will lead to adulting well in others. Isn't that hopeful news? Personal growth is very economical and efficient!

The best book I have ever read on grit or perseverance is Angela Duckworth's book *Grit: The Power of Passion and Perseverance*. I won't give a book review because you can get one online, but I will tell you that grit is loosely defined as self-control and stick-to-it-tive-ness. I have been thinking about how necessary grit is, how vital a launching skill it truly is, because this is what Duckworth shares about the research on grit: Grit is more important than skill or education in reaching one's goals and in determining success. Read that sentence again: **Grit is more important than skill or education in reaching one's goals and in determining success.**

Following are Duckworth's four qualities and steps that are necessary in honing grit.

1. Identify a burning interest.

What really lights a fire in you? As you launch into adulthood it might just be getting a job that pays enough to support yourself. It might be getting a graduate education. It could be as simple as being a better sibling, friend, or partner. It could be caring for the earth, building bridges with people of other faiths, or making beautiful music. It might be encouraging health and wellness, knitting an afghan, or helping the homeless. Whatever it is, identify your burning interest. Many goals are not reached because they are made without a guiding, burning desire.

2. Practice it a lot.

There just is no substitute for practice. We all need hours spent learning, repeating, and developing the necessary skills to put our passion into action. Most things worthwhile do not come easily. They come with sweat equity. So practice, practice, and then practice some more. Another way to think about this is that you'll need to get some wind in your sails. It will not benefit you to frequently change direction. Slow down and stick with something long enough to learn some important skills and develop some expertise.

Grit is not about instant gratification. It's about sticking with it when you run into a wall, when your friends or parents say discouraging things, or when the reward seems a long way away. It's about sticking with it when you don't get the recognition you believe you deserve. Grit is long hours, sweat, paying your dues, crying in frustration, and making it through the mile-stone you never thought you would. It's about creative problem solving and finding new ways to get where you want to go. When you hit a rough patch, buckle down. Double your efforts. You gotta have something real to put on that resume!

How do you get to Carnegie Hall?
Practice, Practice, Practice
—origins unknown

3. **Have a sense that whatever you are working on will contribute to making the world a better place.**

Many social scientists believe that we are born with a desire to help others. Deep inside each of us, we truly want to make a change, to see our efforts making the world a better place. Examine your thoughts about this. When we are helpful in a way that really matters, the energy allows us to keep trying hard and to stick with something. If your burning interest is to get a job and pay your bills, that is okay, because doing that actually does make the world a better place. One more adult doing what adults should do: taking personal responsibility for life. You might consider, though, how achieving your goal is bigger than just you.

4. **Rid yourself of pessimism and develop a growth mindset.**

You can learn optimism (ask for help with this if you need it!), and it truly does make a difference in the outcome of your efforts. There's actually a worthwhile book by Martin Seligman called *Learned Optimism.* So stopping your negative thinking and instead believing that you will improve will hone personal grit.

Let me use myself as an example of these four qualities. I love the fields of psychology and spirituality, and I love the way they complement each other and the ways they intersect. I can talk about them for hours. So I would consider practicing psychotherapy, blogging, and writing about this a burning desire. Nailed the first quality of developing grit.

About practicing. Practicing is sometimes known as **the 10,000-hour rule**. According to Malcolm Gladwell, author of *Outliers*, you have to do something for 10,000 hours before you are considered an expert. Or as my late piano teacher, Louella Gibson, used to say, "For every time you play that incorrectly, Amy, you have to play it correctly seven times." Therefore, it is important while developing grit to practice correctly. Slow down. Do it right. Log your hours. I do have a lot of practice in psychology and spirituality. And I probably have 10,000 hours of blogging and authoring by now. Are you putting in the necessary time to build a habit? To increase your skill level? To develop grit? You'd be surprised how quickly those hours add up. Keep practicing! You'll get there.

Do I believe healthy psychology and good spirituality will make the world a better place? Do I believe this little book can help? Hell, yes! I believe people need skills, and you, you who are trying so hard to launch, you might be helped by this book. Some of the people we interviewed while writing this book told us how helpful it would be and encouraged us. So I am good at Step 3. Please ask yourself these questions. Is whatever it is you are trying to accomplish going to make the world a better place? How will holding on to a job and supporting yourself make the world a better place? How will learning to be a better partner make the world a better place? I am serious. Work it through in your head—or on a concept map. Maybe it will help your family? Your friends? Your community? What will you **do** with your ability to work and pay your bills? With your new-found relationship skills? Sometimes this is called "finding your why."

Do I have a growth mindset, part of Step 4? I can tell you that when it came to writing this book, I struggled. I was not rid of pessimism. And you know what Rhea and I did? **We asked for help. Yes, we actually practice what we preach. And it worked!** We went back to Skill #1 [Ask for Help]. We got the name of an editor and had a Zoom meeting with her. She was so encouraging. So hopeful. She "got us" right away and buoyed us up and had a laser vision for us when we only had a blurry vision for ourselves. It was fabulous. That meeting shifted everything. The optimism and vision we had when the call was over swung us into high gear and we've been working and writing ever since. Optimism and a growth mindset are two virtues that will help you hone your own grit and reach your highest goals.

Don't be pushed around by the fears in your mind. Be led by the dreams in your heart.
—Roy T. Bennett, *The Light In The Heart*

Have you seen the movie *Hidden Figures?* It was nominated for a number of Academy Awards in 2016, and I hope you will watch it if you haven't already. This is a movie about many people with grit, but especially about three women who had an exponential amount of grit and finally made history because of that grit. One of my favorite scenes in the movie is when actress Janelle Monae as Mary Jackson, an African American mathematician working at NASA in the 1960s, goes in front of a judge to ask for access to classes that were only offered in a whites-only segregated high school. She needed the classes to become an engineer. She did not go and whine to the judge about how she should be let in or how wrong segregation was. She did her research, knew her audience (the judge), played to his own interests, and was granted access. This woman had grit!!! All three of the women highlighted in this biographical drama had extraordinary grit.

45

So what is it that you really want to achieve? Can you hold up what you really want to these four qualities of grit, take an honest look to see where you are good, and where you may need to work harder? It's worth being intentional about this if you really want to get where you say you want to go!

Adulting is getting messier and more marvelous by the minute, Friends. Join us in developing personal grit and keep the marvelous happening.

LAUNCH Questions for Reflection and Discussion

Can you name a burning desire?

What is your current tolerance for failure? What messages have you received in the past about failing? What is your response to failure right now? Be specific.

How good are you at tolerating discomfort? At delaying gratification and waiting for a reward?

Name a time in your life when you did persist and achieved a goal. Break it down. What worked? What steps did you take to reach your goal? Now pick an important long-term goal. Break it down. What step comes next?

Notes:

LAUNCH Checklist

☐ Journal Tip: Write about any dreams and desires you have. Include a short-term dream (within the next year) and a long-term dream (5–10 years). Think in terms of how you would like to create your life in both the near and the farther future. **AND, remember to name your why! Why** is this a dream of yours?

☐ Get yourself an accountability partner. Set goals and ask this partner to be the person who holds you accountable for your persistence. This person could be a friend or a professional coach.

☐ Break a large task into smaller goals. Reward yourself for small achievements along the way.

☐ Create a vision board or use a bullet journal. Search YouTube: Jack Canfield how to create a vision board. www.bulletjournal.com (There's an App for that.)

LAUNCH Resources

* *Grit: The Power of Passion and Perseverance,* by Angela Duckworth

* *Learned Optimism,* by Martin Seligman

* Podcast: *A Bit Of Optimism,* by Simon Sinek

* The American Psychological Association has pages on how to build resilience: https://www.apa.org/topics/resilience

Love and compassion are necessities, not luxuries.
Without them, humanity cannot survive.

—Dalai Lama

Reserve Judgment— Find Compassion

by *Rhea*

The judging mind is an interesting thing. When we see failure in others or when we fail, our judging mind quickly has a lot to say and it's not usually positive. Like the saying, "Your mind is an unsafe neighborhood; don't go there alone," the dark alleys in our heads are often unkind places. When our initial reflex is to judge, the challenge is to choose to practice compassion, both for ourselves and for others. Let me share three stories, all from one week, that highlight our instinct to judge, and the gift of connection when, instead, we choose to respond with curiosity and compassion.

One bright fall day, I lingered over lunch with friends and colleagues, enjoying stories and banter. One woman told of a lifetime achievement award speech given by a leader in her field some years before. What stayed with my friend was how the speaker discussed his successes and yet skillfully wove in his personal story of a lifelong struggle with depression. She was so impressed that she stayed to speak with him after the talk and to share a bit of her own mental health struggle. She was impressed that someone of such notoriety shared what some might consider "a failure." What stayed with me after our lunch was how important his vulnerable revelation was to her.

Later that afternoon, while perusing social media, I saw an article about a man who had been an Ivy League-educated, successful entrepreneur who was living penniless on the streets of Los Angeles. His story was the target of federal criticism about increased homelessness and ineffective solutions by many municipalities. If we're being honest, many of us have stereotypical judgments about people who are homeless and we are critical and uncomfortable about this serious problem in our cities. We look away and attempt to distance ourselves by walking away feeling self-satisfied.

The same week, an article came across my desk about a college counseling center director who died by suicide after six months in his new position. He, too, was a lifetime achievement award winner. Having worked in a college counseling center, and as a psychologist myself, I was stunned and heartbroken—although I never knew this man. But what is the most common thing people say after the news of a suicide? "It's so selfish"—a declaration that promotes stigma and helps us distance ourselves from that desperate place inside of us at times. Rather than judging his final act, I found myself curious about what led him there. I'm sure I am among many of his friends, family, and colleagues who wish they could ask him more.

Be kind, for everyone you meet is fighting a hard battle.
—Ian Maclaren

These stories illustrate the notion that no one is exempt from hardship or the messy side of life. Because of my work, I am much more aware of how often someone can appear fine publicly when they are suffering privately. **Success does not make anyone immune to hardship.** But in each of these situations, many of us might be quick to judge which serves to distance us from discomfort and from the people that we don't understand. It goes something like this:

Judgment → Criticism → Distance

A part of this problem of judgment is that we tend to look at others through our own lens. So how do we move from judging to compassion? I believe it begins with curiosity and could look like this:

Curiosity → Compassion → Connection

To illustrate this, I worked with a mother who had a grown daughter who was struggling with the basic responsibilities of adulting following her college graduation. I listened to her worry and distress over her child and yet when she recounted their interactions, I heard the mother's verbal criticism that undermined her profound concern. When faced with her mother's judging attitude, the daughter defended herself with verbal hostility, avoidance, and, ultimately, distance. My interventions focused on how the mother might communicate with more empathy and curiosity about why her daughter's path had so abruptly derailed in the past year.

Be curious, not judgmental.
—Walt Whitman

I am confident that this mother loved her daughter dearly and was trying to help her be successful. But her efforts were backfiring. If she were to communicate curiosity rather than criticism, it would convey compassion and, "I want to understand you." When curiosity and compassion are the messages, we create a stronger connection.

So what makes finding compassion an important adulting skill?

One definition of compassion is a "sympathetic consciousness of others' distress **together with a desire to alleviate it**" (Merriam-Webster online).

According to this definition, it is more than a feeling; there is also an action involved. An intention without action creates or changes very little. The desire to alleviate another's distress gives us greater meaning and purpose in this life. It builds connections with others. A judging and critical attitude separates us from others, both individually and in our community.

A little story about how a knee-jerk judgment can obscure our compassion: Imagine that you are driving down the road and a car barrels down upon you, tailgates, swerving back and forth across lanes, then blasts erratically around you. First reaction? *Shaking fist* + *"@$$#0££!"* It's easy to jump to the conclusion that the person is just a jerk. So you step on the gas, race up beside the driver to give them a *"loud non-verbal message,"* and you see that the man is wearing a turban-like wrap around his head. Now what do you think? Perhaps now, suspicious of his motives, you drop back and decide to follow him. The guy pulls into the hospital emergency entrance, jumps out of the car in a bloodied shirt, and calls for help. The hospital personnel arrive and take two children, of an obviously different race than the man, out of the backseat, and rush them in on a gurney. What do you think now? The man then sits down on the curb, head in his hands, crying until a nurse brings a wheelchair and takes him inside.

Now what do you think?

As much as I strive to practice acceptance in my therapy office, like anyone, I can be awfully "judgy" in my personal life. It's the side of me I don't like and continually work on. But my efforts can only be focused on the judgments about which I am aware. There are also the judgments of which we are often unaware. Known as "implicit bias," we all have unconscious stereotypes, attitudes, and prejudices that lead us to swift judgment without stopping to think. Like the story of the erratic driver, we make many quick assumptions before we have all of the information. If we stop at our first, knee-jerk judgment, we will likely miss the most important information—the very information that may guide us toward compassion and connection.

Do you want to know the end of the story about the erratic, bloodied driver? In fact, he witnessed an accident and stopped to help. Another bystander called 911 but the dispatcher said a traffic jam was going to substantially delay the ambulance. The man realized that his route to the hospital was clear and that he could have the children there in minutes. So, what do you feel now about this man that is different from your first reaction before you knew the whole story?

In this messy, messy world, how do you respond to people or situations that leave you feeling uncomfortable? What happens when you hear the story of a vulnerable colleague? What do you say to yourself about someone living on the streets? How do you judge a desperate, depressed man? What happens in your gut when you see someone in unfamiliar dress? How do you respond to a person who seems erratic? How do you talk to your own loved one who is not doing what is expected? Do you jump to conclusions and make judgments from the safety of what you believe you know? Or do you remain curious until you have the whole story? Do you stay open to more information in an attempt to connect your experience to something unfamiliar? Are you able to offer compassion first?

Here's the thing: People are messy. Connections with others are messy. The world is messy. Adulting is messy and calls for us to not be too quick to distance ourselves by making a quick judgment and reacting with criticism. Imagine a world in which we choose to reserve judgment and, instead, find ways to connect with others through curiosity and compassion. Imagine a day without judging yourself but rather, practicing self-compassion. What a day that would be. *Marvelous!*

LAUNCH Questions for Reflection and Discussion

What is your level of self-awareness regarding who and what you judge? In other words, is your judgment based on a fear? A failing? A dislike of something?

How often do you find yourself with a critical narrative in your head? Are you willing to begin to listen carefully to your own critical thoughts?

There's a saying: "Don't judge another until you have walked a mile in their shoes." How will you work to develop curiosity toward other peoples' stories and struggles?

How willing are you to put in some spiritual and mental effort to challenge your judgy self? Are you willing to go to the extra effort to advocate for someone who is in need of compassion?

LAUNCH checklist:

☐ Journal Tip: Practice writing compassionate messages of kindness for people with whom you are struggling.

☐ There is a meditation technique called "tonglen meditation." Contrary to many meditation breathing techniques, you breathe in another's pain and breathe out loving-kindness. Find it here: https://www.lionsroar.com/how-to-practice-tonglen/

☐ Sit down with someone you tend to find yourself negatively judging. Practice asking questions from a place of curiosity and wonder. Examples of good questions might be: Can you help me understand that more? What led you to this belief or decision? What is at stake for you?

LAUNCH Resources

- *Radical Compassion: Learning To Love Yourself and Your World With The Practice Of RAIN*, by Tara Brach

- Podcast: *Tara Brach*

- *The Compassion Book: Teaching For Awakening The Heart,* by Pema Chodron

- Podcast: *Oprah's Super Soul Sunday October 23,2019: Welcoming The Unwelcome*

- In the App store: *CompassionToday!*

A dream you dream alone is only a dream.
A dream you dream together is reality.

—John Lennon

We are like islands in the sea, separate on the surface but connected in the deep.

—William James

Find Your People

by *Rhea*

It had been a long week and I had been invited to a Friday night birthday party for a friend. I thought I would stay a couple of hours, or less. As it turned out, and not surprising for this extrovert, the host locked up behind me and a couple of other last-to-leave stragglers late in the night. What kept me there, despite my initial resistance, was the intimate conversation. The host and I had been in yoga class together for more years than either one of us cared to count but we had never taken time to have a true conversation.

During the conversation, he mentioned that he had a group of male friends who get together once a month—*not* to play poker or hunt. They gather to talk, share, and support one another. Ten men. Some of them have known each other for decades, and some were new friends they brought in over time. Each month, one of the men hosts and picks a topic for conversation. It might be a dilemma, a struggle, or a curiosity in life. They share and support each other. Then once a year, they go on a week-long retreat together in the mountains. They call themselves the Step-brothers, and my friend said he couldn't imagine his life without them.

What this man was telling me was that he had found his people. The group of people with whom he could be his most authentic self. The people he turned to for help when needed. The group who helped hold him accountable to be his best self. The group who reflect back to him so he can better know himself. The men with whom he practices compassion without judgment.

Sounds enviable, huh?

Another very meaningful conversation I enjoyed that same Friday evening was with a fellow I just love more and more every time I have the privilege of being around him. He shared about his mission and work with a not-for profit healing center for military vets. Having worked in combat zones himself, he rediscovered his own life and healing from combat PTSD through art and community. Now a professional photographer, he continues to help groups of Vets heal by discovering their own creativity.

Healing comes from sharing.
—Messy Marvelous

Avoid Isolation

In contrast, we know that isolation kills. I don't mean the selective isolation of a quiet Saturday morning when the family is away briefly. Or the decision to go on a solo retreat. Those are times that our bodies, brains, and souls need a rest from the busy-ness of life. I'm referring to those who don't believe they have (or really don't have) anyone to whom they can turn in times of stress or when in need of support and companionship.

I recently read a telling bit of research by Dr. John Gottman in his book, *The Relationship Cure*. He writes about a study at Yale University of 10,000 college seniors who identified themselves as "loners." A five-year follow-up discovered that they had a two-times higher risk of *dying from all causes* than those who claimed to have close friendships. A startling finding for the young and typically healthy. Similarly, a study in England of men and women over the age of 52 found that loneliness and the associated mechanism, social isolation, significantly increased risk of death from all causes in seven years.

My young friends and former students who are in their twenties and early thirties say that finding their community of people is one of the greatest challenges in their newly minted adult lives. Leaving school and the proximity of friends can be difficult. When asked, they unanimously offered as a priority the importance of finding community. And that it is hard. As one noted, "You can't just walk out of your door and see who is available to hang out." It takes much more intention, whether to make an initial connection, or to stay connected.

These young, wise people also shared the value they see in finding friends who are different. New friends who bring differences to the relationship. Someone to challenge their thinking. People of different ages and stages who opened up new worlds. There's something to be learned from everyone. These young people are treasures in my life and I feel honored to be included in theirs.

Stay Connected—It's Worth the Effort

Relationships evolve. And establishing these close relationships takes time. Sometimes a long time. I met one of my dearest friends about 20 years ago. She was in a yoga class with me for a couple of years when one of my other friends began to establish a relationship with her. I followed suit. Within a few years we began to have lunches, then drinks, then dinners, followed down the road by holiday parties, and later, birthday parties with the "inner circle," and now intimate family holidays, late-night raps, confiding about our deepest heartbreaks, and celebrating long-awaited joys.

These types of relationships are rare. This is the friend who calls you first thing in the morning when you're freshly separated and lonely, just to help you feel connected. This is the friend who brings your favorite dish following surgery without asking. This is the friend who buys you something beautiful that she saw on sale and knew you would love it. This is the friend who meets you to play tennis because he promised he would even though it will mean he has to work late into the night to meet a deadline. This friend will show up, tell hard truths, and continue to love you.

Knowing full well I am not a morning person, a friend I'd had for twenty years called me very early one morning to tell me that she was extremely sick. Without another word, I said, "I'll be right there. Unlock your door." Still in my pajamas, I threw on a coat and shoes and raced out the door to her home, making a plan for which emergency room I would drive her to based on the likelihood of a shorter wait time. I got her in the car without debating if she should go or not because she had crawled to the front door and was lying next to it waiting for me. After we arrived and she was triaged, the staff insisted that she sit in the waiting room. She could neither walk nor sit, doubled over in pain but they could not, or would not, spare a gurney for her to lie on until she could be seen. In the waiting area, I put my coat on the floor for her to lie on without a second to consider the status of the hospital linoleum (ew!). We garnered quite a few puzzled or critical looks as she laid there, curled up like a cat, on my coat on the floor of the hospital emergency department floor with me hovering—in my pj's. Maybe, just maybe, her need and my deep concern got her seen sooner.

She celebrates our connection when she laughingly tells others that not many friends would let you lie on the hospital floor on their coat. I know that beneath her comedic telling of the story, her message is one of gratitude—a tribute to our closeness and many years together. I am very fortunate to have her, Amy, and a few others who make up my heart family and who I can call anytime. Just as any one of them would lay their coat down for me, you, too, can count on that with those in your community of people.

There's another piece of the puzzle here as well. Are you familiar with the popular phrase, "Like attracts like?" You might also have to try being the kind of person you want to be in order to attract a community of people! If you want to attract interesting, caring, fun, loving people to be a close community, be interesting, caring, fun, and loving. You can do this!

Adulting is messy. We all experience hardships. Hardships that are only made harder if you don't have a support network, or if you are experiencing profound loneliness. So find your like-minded folks, your people, your heart-family. And remember to look for people who don't look, think, or believe like you. Stay connected. Share the stories of your life. Share experiences. Your people help you hang on and discover the Marvelous.

LAUNCH Questions for Reflection and Consideration

What would it be like to join an interest group where you have no existing connection to anyone? Would you do it?

Are you willing to be the initiator, the inviter, for an outing or a get-together?

What stories are in your head that become obstacles when trying to connect with others?

If you already have a community of people, what characteristics make it important to you? If you haven't found your people, what are you looking for?

LAUNCH Checklist

☐ Journal Tip: Write about a time when you most felt a part of something. Focus on how that got started and how it ended (if it did). List the messages you tell yourself about that experience.

☐ Pick someone you have an interest in getting to know better. Ask them to join you for a cup of coffee or a drink in order to get to know them better. Call people back and invite them AGAIN, even if they've turned you down more than once.

☐ Write a lovely, heartfelt snail mail thank-you note when someone has invited you to something.

☐ Join a group that is focused around an activity you enjoy.

LAUNCH Resources

The TedTalk: "Falling in Love is the Easy Part" by Mandy Lee Catron is really not about falling in love, but how to ask questions that foster closeness. Google "the 36 questions" for more.

Here to Make Friends: How to Make Friends as an Adult, by Hope Kelaher

Engage in "Big Talk": See Kalina Silverman's TEDxWestminster called, "How to Skip Small Talk and Connect with Anyone" and her website at www.MakeBigTalk.com for more.

There are two kinds of people in this world, the givers and the takers. The takers sometimes eat better, but the givers always sleep better.

—attributed to Danny Thomas

Reach Out and Give Back

by *Amy*

Okay, you're finding your people. You have a group of besties. Your heart is feeling full. So far, this adulting stuff is going pretty well. You are moving beyond just surviving now, and it's actually starting to feel like you are thriving. You pick up your head, look around, and realize the world needs you.

Let me tell you a story. I was fortunate to be raised by parents who gave back to their communities in so many ways. Generous giving was modeled for me. So when I went off to Furman University in Greenville, South Carolina, one of the first things I did was sign up to work in the Collegiate Education Service Corps (CESC). My volunteer work began in Greenville's city mini-parks, parks that were placed in low-income neighborhoods where kids might not otherwise have safe places to play with adult supervision and guidance. I went once a week for a few hours, played with the children, talked with them, and frequently brought a snack for them. During my senior year, out of my love for dance, I felt inspired to start a dance class in one of the parks. I was given permission to use a recreation center and every Saturday morning I had about 15 girls who showed up for a dance class. I loved it. I think it felt as good for me as it did for them.

Forty years later, I was meeting a new client in my office. We made our introductions and sometime in the middle of the session she said to me,

"I feel like I know you." At first it felt a little weird because it didn't seem possible. I sure didn't know her. We followed that thread for a minute. … Where did you grow up? *Greenville.* I was in Greenville for a while. I went to Furman. *I lived in this neighborhood.* Hmmmm. … I worked in that neighborhood with the service corps. Bright eyes. *You taught dance in the rec center.* Yes I did. *Your classes mattered so much to me. They gave me something to look forward to each week.*

HOLY WOW. The lesson, as always, is this: You never know how what you do or how you live is going to affect somebody. Forty years later, I relived the joy in having given back. And, another lesson: I would not have been able to give back without having joined CESC. Joining this organization gave me the opportunity to reach out and give back. I could not have done it on my own.

We are social beings. When we give back to others, we release what some people call the "Happiness Trifecta": serotonin, dopamine, and oxytocin. Each of these brain chemicals work in different ways, but giving to others releases all three at once. So, giving is good for you. That might be reason enough for some of you. More happiness? Absolutely. Give back.

On a deeper level, if you want to go there with me, is the wisdom from every major religion and philosophy. Giving back gives more meaning to life. It is the other half of receiving. There is a circuit—we receive and we give, we give and we receive. If only one part of this circuit is flowing, the circuit isn't able to complete its cycle. We must learn to give AND we must learn to receive. I like the idea of the giving of my "time, talent, and treasure," a phrase I learned in The Episcopal Church. If you are short on ideas of ways to give back, there's a long list at the end of this chapter. But please don't feel limited by it. Your ideas are as good as mine!

Evolutionary scientists say we are born to belong. Before industrialization, not belonging—to the tribe, the community, the village, the family—actually meant death. The need to join together was the only way possible to survive. Additionally, the need to give to others, to invest in another's well-being, is vital, not only to our human survival, but also to our *human nature*. Our brains and our souls are better when we give back. Organizational psychologist Adam Grant, in his book *Give and Take*, shares research that shows that work places also thrive when there are more givers than takers on staff.

Remember, we humans are naturally social beings. One of the things that can make high school and college some of the best years of life is that you have a built-in, immediately available community. When you go back to the dorm, Greek village, or your apartment, your friends are right there. Someone is usually available to talk, play video games, go out to lunch, drink coffee, study, watch TV, go for a run, or just eat a bucket of popcorn with you. It's pretty awesome. And if someone isn't right there, they usually aren't far away. They may be in the library, office, coffee shop, lab, bar, gym, or laundry area, but close they are! You have ready-made opportunities for community that you can access with little effort.

It bears repeating from Skill #6: Find Your People, that this is one of the biggest changes and challenges when you launch. Your friends may not be right there. They may be in another city or state. They may just be busy with new jobs or even new families. Those community outreach projects that were designed for you by your "group" are no longer as easy to access. You may lose all the extra-curricular "groups" you so loved and counted on for friendship and social engagement. It can leave you feeling pretty lonely and isolated and spending way too much time online, which is a poor substitute for real-life connections.

Time to figure out how to reach out and what to join. The opportunities are endless but they won't come to you. You have to go to them. This could be a very long list (See the end of this chapter for some ideas if you need help getting started.). The point is, it will take some initiative and effort from you. And it is really important to learn to do this, even if it is initially awkward.

Let me tell you another story, this one about two friends of mine, a couple in their thirties. She moved to her husband's town and home when they married. She also began to work from home, which she had never done before. It was feeling pretty lonely, even though the marriage was great and they enjoyed spending time together. After a little brain-storming, they decided to start having a weekly dinner at their house, and invited a few neighbors and a few friends. They make the main meal and others bring something to add. It is now a night everyone looks forward to, and it is helping her with a sense of connection. A beautiful addition is that her husband, a math and money whiz, is teaching and coaching one of the others in the area of money management (Skill #9) because that person said they needed help with money (Skill #1), and this is a way my friend feels like he is giving back (Skill #7)! So many skills sharpened with one creative act of reaching out and joining. Well done!

So reaching out is vital. Giving back brings joy. But none of this is easy.

Adulting is messy. Don't go it alone. Reach out, give back, and make this messy world a little more marvelous.

LAUNCH Questions for Reflection and Discussion

Mary Oliver says, "Give until the giving feels like receiving."* Have you had an experience of giving back until it felt like receiving?

How would you describe the difference between receiving and taking?

Look back at the opening quote in this skill: "There are two kinds of people in the world, the givers and the takers." Which are you? Are you different in different circumstances?

Is there an organization that you would be willing to give to? If you could give in the form of time, talent, or money, which are you more likely to do, or comfortable offering?

Notes:

LAUNCH Checklist

☐ Journal Tip: Write honestly about your propensity for giving and taking. Consider ways to have a more balanced approach to life, honing both your receiving and giving skills.

☐ Pick an organization that shares your beliefs and vision for an issue. Find a way to get involved. At the minimum, make financial donations.

☐ The word "allyship" has made its way into our vocabulary. It denotes an active participation and an accompanying of a minority or marginalized person or group. Pick a person or group and focus on how to become an ally.

LAUNCH Resources

Adam Grant's (author of *Originals*) Tedtalk: https://www.ted.com/talks/adam_grant_are_you_a_giver_or_a_taker?language=en

Tony Robbins' blog: https://www.tonyrobbins.com/giving-back/importance-giving-back/

The Giving Back Guidebook For Young Professionals, by Joanna Blanding

Some Ideas of Ways to Give Back

1. Find a volunteer position with an organization you truly care about.

2. Read to a younger child.

3. Sign-up for auto-debit with some non-profits. (You won't even miss the money!)

4. Tithe to a church, or other religious or spiritual organization of your choice.

5. Teach someone else something you are good at (cooking, knitting, golf, yoga, wood-working, etc.).

6. Raise money for a cause you believe in.

7. Help a friend accomplish a task they hate (organizing a closet, painting a room, filing their taxes).

8. Smile at the cashier. Better yet, offer a kind word with that smile.

9. Practice a random act of kindness.

10. Pray for someone else.

11. Be a team coach, a scout leader, a big-brother or sister, a generous friend.

12. Add your own: _____

Some Ideas of Things to Reach Out to or Join

1. Find intramural sports teams, available in nearly every city.

2. Go to the local library and join a book club.

3. Find your political party's local headquarters and get involved.

4. Find a civic chorus, band, or orchestra to join.

5. Visit churches and invest in the one you feel most comfortable in.

6. Start your own supper club.

7. Talk to your neighbors. See what they are involved in.

8. Find the young adult's group at the local museum.

9. Find a trivial pursuit team, or Magic card team

10. Join a hiking, kayaking, star-gazing, outdoorsy kind of group.

11. Pick a gym, yoga or Pilates studio, boxing club, and go at the same time until you meet the other people who go at the same time.

12. Audition for the civic theatre, or work backstage

13. Add your own: _____

Relationship is true when two partners adjust for each other, support each other, stand for each other, and most importantly, let each other be free to live the life they love.

—Urvashi Vats

Partner Each Other

by *Rhea*

Amy and I have been friends for about three decades, and we've probably talked about every relationship topic possible. As our children have reached their late 20s and early 30s, one common quandary we often discuss is how different their lives are from our lives at these respective ages. The biggest difference is that Amy and I both married young—before or shortly after graduating college, and by the age of 30, we were both mothers. Not the case for our collective three—only one is married, although the other two live with their partners, and there are no grandchildren yet. Keenly aware that there are advantages and disadvantages in each pattern of relationship formation, we've discussed the nuance of growing up then partnering (our children) vs. partnering and then growing each other up (us). Again—one is not better than the other. Just different.

What is not different is what happens when we make a decision to braid our life together with someone else's. We find ourselves in many dilemmas about how to do that. How much autonomy do we retain? How do we communicate about our togetherness and our separateness? How do we merge our two lives and things into the life of a couple? How do we settle disagreements or differences in personal tastes? How do we mix our money?

I've reflected on how these questions also apply to second marriages or dating in midlife. In both cases, this a-bit-later-in-life partnering seems to center on finding someone who is well-matched in terms of how closely we can fit our lives onto a similar path. I recently found myself engaging in a discussion with a couple who were asking these same kinds of questions. The husband asked to be coached to do a better job at merging his life with his partner's.

In a relationship, each person should support each other; they should lift each other up. —Taylor Swift

I'm not sure if this client knew this or not, but part of my work is with athletes and teams. In some sports, like swimming, gymnastics, tennis, or equestrian, individuals compete for the sake of an overall team victory. A single competitor might win an event, yet the team might still lose. In a true team sport, like basketball or soccer, if one player scores, the team scores. Team spirit can be easy to build in this type of team. In the individual sports, however, it can be challenging to build a sense of cohesiveness among the team members.

I was struck by how this also can be true with some couples who may be competing for space in a relationship. If I've been winning in my life, and you've been winning in yours, how do we merge our two paths? Many times, marriage or life partnership means that someone takes a supportive role while the other focuses on a career goal. Hopefully, partners can take turns being in the supportive role.

One wise senior equestrian spoke up in a team building exercise and said, "Honestly, I'd love to be competing but I don't know if I'll get that chance; if not, I'll happily shovel shit or whatever. I'll be there to cheer on whoever ends up in the spot I wanted. Because if they win, we all win; and I'll have a national championship ring whether I compete or not."

Sitting with the couple who wanted to be coached, I couldn't help but notice the striking difference in how she went to great effort to support him to be successful, which he openly acknowledged, but when the question was turned back to him, he admitted that he felt competitive with her. Like a good coach, I tried to give him play options. We practiced ways that he might be supportive of her successes. I tried to help him see that if she wins, he wins.

Love is a game two can play and both win. —Eva Gabor

Marriage or a partnership with another person is about give and take. We've all heard that and in theory, it sounds easy. Until it's your time to give up something. More than likely, that's when fear takes over. It is very difficult to connect as a partner when you're filled with fear. Think of it like trying to connect with a roaring lion. No thanks. We have to look deep inside to figure out why we might feel hesitant to support our partner.

And what about those two separate, carefully crafted, successful lives? What's the plan for the merger? When two businesses merge, **every. single. detail.** is carefully examined, outlined, and reviewed by all parties (and their attorneys). But love can be blind and I think that, many times, people just dive into marriage without looking at their expectations around important issues, such as time together and time apart, money, children, workloads, household responsibilities, extended family, and so on. A business would never take such considerations for granted simply because the other business was successful and had good curb appeal. No way.

So maybe among the discussions of where we want to have our wedding and in what season, we also should engage in premarital counseling where we can discuss things, like what we think a good partner does for the other. Where we can really examine how we give support and how we want to receive support. What can we give up? What can we not imagine sacrificing? What are our deal-breakers? How much togetherness and separateness can we tolerate? How will money be saved, spent, and given charitably? What are sexual expectations? How do we handle holidays? What about our extended families?

Finally, I would add that to decide to live your life without a partner is a perfectly valid choice, regardless of what your grandmother may think. But even still, many people find it necessary to live with someone else--a friend, a roommate you don't know well, a sibling or single parent, or even in a co-housing arrangement. These co-living arrangements also go more smoothly when we examine lifestyle preferences, expectations, and the division of responsibilities. Or maybe you want to be a good partner in a friendship. Being able to navigate expectations, closeness and distance, or how we support one another are important conversations when our friendships seem to become messy.

Life has a lot of messy turns and we will really need each other on this road of life. Ask yourself: How can I be a marvelous partner? How can I be the best team member possible so we can get a win in this big messy, and yet marvelous, game?

LAUNCH Questions for Reflection and Discussion

What are some ways you show support to your partner? What actions do you take to help them be successful in their life?

Do you ever feel hesitant to throw your support behind your partner's dreams? List some of the thoughts, feelings, and/or fears that create barriers to offering your full support?

What are your expectations of your partner as you merge your lives? What are you willing to sacrifice? What could you never give up?

Notes:

LAUNCH Checklist

☐ Journal Tip: Write about how you view a long-term relationship. Include how you imagine daily life and what prevents you from fulfilling those dreams. Identify the patterns that get in your way and how you might begin by making small changes.

☐ Sit with your partner and make separate lists of hopes and wishes, both the day-to-day kind and longer-term dreams. Compare lists.

☐ Practice the art of listening and understanding your partner at a deeper level.

LAUNCH Resources

7 Principles for Making Marriage Work, by John Gottman. This is not just a book for married people, but a sound communication guide for anyone in a relationship

Gottman Card Decks app, 14 in all for working on your relationship

Love Sense, by Sue Johnson

The New Rules of Marriage, by Terrance Real. And anything else by him you can get your hands on

Similarly, anything by Esther Perel: her books, podcasts, and her TedTalks

Wealth consists not in having great possessions, but in having few wants.

—Epictetus

Manage Your Money

by *Amy*

Money, sex, religion, and politics. Apparently these are the four most difficult topics to talk about. For those of you launching into the adult world, money might be the most difficult topic of those four. Learning to make money, to budget and live within the money you make, to manage debt, to educate yourself about the world of money, and to manage the anxiety around money—all of this takes skill worthy of your effort. Hang in there with me. This is an important topic and that's why this is a little long.

What does money mean to you?

Money represents many things. It can be a symbol of status, power, freedom, sensibilities, and generosity. It can buy recreational activities, cultural activities, and, sometimes, it can even buy friends. Or relationships. So when we talk about money, there are usually some deep-seated feelings present. "I deserve this. I want this. I need this. I am tired of being broke. This will change my life. This will make me happy." Money is closely tied to survival needs, and so at our core, we all have issues around money. You're not alone.

If you've been dependent on your parent's financial support, the launching step of living by your own means might be a gradual one.

If you have an entry-level job somewhere, it is likely that living independently and supporting yourself will seem impossible. Between your rent, utilities, car insurance, perhaps a car payment, phone bill, taxes, and student loans, your paycheck might already be gone. How will you ever have enough to do some fun things? To vacation? To date? And what happens when your car breaks down? The temptation to take on more debt is palpable. The temptation to bury your head in the sand may be even stronger.

If you are in graduate school and the student debt is looming larger than ever, the heaviness of debt and the pessimism of thinking you will never get out from under it can be paralyzing. There are ways, however, of learning to live within your means and of having a plan to manage when you get out "on your own."

Where and how do I start?

Advice from anyone with whom you consult will begin with the task of making a budget. It's not as difficult as it sounds. For a couple of months, keep a running record of every penny you spend. You could do it the old-fashioned way, with papyrus and quill, (a small notebook on the counter where you log each day what was spent), you could find an App, or you could just keep up with it in your phone. However you do it, be completely honest. Every. Single. Penny. At the end of two months, add up what you spent in various categories. Rent, groceries, transportation, utilities, phone, eating out, entertainment, medical, health and wellness, clothing, travel. … You get the idea. Then, take a look at your paycheck and see where you are. Overspending? Under budget?

Money often costs too much.
—Ralph Waldo Emerson

If you are shocked and horrified at one of these categories, start regrouping. I remember the last time I re-evaluated my budget and was shocked at how much I spent on food and wine. I remember re-calculating, sure that I had pushed the wrong number on the calculator a few times. Nope. My husband and I were spending $800 a month on food and wine. Too much for our budget. We started regrouping. Less expensive wine. Less meat. I hear from people all the time when they do this exercise that they are usually shocked by how much they spend eating out, or on coffee-shop coffee. A barista recently told me that several of the customers who frequent her store spend $300–400 dollars a month there. Yikes. Yes, it all adds up.

There are all kinds of online banks and apps to help with that. One of my favorites is "Simple." It allows you to take your money, deposit it, put it in electronic "envelopes" according to your budget, and then when you want to spend, it will tell you whether there is enough money in that envelope to spend or not. Immediate feedback. You can move money from one envelope to another, but the point is that there is a finite amount of money and when it's gone, it's gone. It's the technological equivalent to my parents who used actual envelopes with actual cash in them back in the 1960s. My father would cash his weekly paycheck, give it to my mom, who would then divvy it up into the food, church, school supplies, and clothing envelopes. When it was gone, it was gone.

An Irrational Suggestion

Now I want to suggest something that might sound very old-fashioned and perhaps controversial. I remain certain about this, though, which is why I am putting it in here. I want to suggest that when you get your money, before you divvy it up according to your budget, you put 10% of that money into a savings account and 10% of that money into the charity of your choice. Whaatt? You are not making enough to live on! How are you going to save and give away money?

I have heard this argument my whole adult life, from friends, clients, colleagues, and others. Here's what I still know and see. If you will get used to doing this, to putting this money aside from the very beginning, you will learn to live on the rest. You will make choices from the very beginning that will allow you to live on the rest. You might buy a less expensive car, take in a roommate, not fly to an unimportant wedding, make do with the clothing you have, workout at home instead of at a gym, make coffee and smoothies yourself, tell your friends you can't go out but they can come over for a game night, make Christmas presents instead of buying them. The list goes on.

What I also know is that you will have a feeling of confidence and safety when you have money in your savings account for a health emergency, a broken vehicle, or a security deposit for an apartment. You will have pride in yourself for being resourceful. You won't have the everlasting angst of debt hanging over your head. You won't be arguing with your parents when you call home for money. Again.

I was sent an article a few years ago by a friend who has always struggled with money. I can't find it now, but in essence the article said that there might actually be a "money gene". She said I had it (the money gene) and she didn't. Apparently some people are good with money because they have the genetic disposition to be and some people just are not lucky that way. I don't know if this is true or not, but the basic idea is that money management comes easier to some than to others. That I think we could all agree on. Even if you don't have the money gene, learning to manage money and live within your means is an important life skill.

A Personal Life Lesson

Back in the days before credit cards were popular, my parents didn't buy anything unless they had saved up for it. There was no such thing as buying something on credit and paying it off. So when our dishwasher was broken for over a year, I had this conversation with my dad as he was washing and I was drying the dinner dishes for the six of us who made up my family.

Me: Dad, why can't we get a new dishwasher? It seems like it's been broken for a long time.

Dad: Oh, we can get a new dishwasher, Honey.

Me: Yay! I am getting sick of washing and drying dishes every night.

Dad: Well, your mother and I will go right out and get one this weekend. That will mean that you cannot go to gymnastics camp or church camp. And your piano lessons might have to stop, too.

Me: WHAAT???? I have to go to gymnastics camp or I won't qualify for the varsity team.

Dad: I guess you'll be washing and drying dishes for a few more months, then.

Life lessons come at teachable moments. Not only was this a lesson in living within one's means, it was a life lesson in priority setting and sacrificial parenting. For the most part, my parents lived within their means and taught me to do the same. Of course credit cards and payment plans have changed the way most of us manage money, and all of that has to be figured out by families and individuals. But in general, the choice to not spend more than one has is a good rule of thumb.

Tame your Wanting Mind

My favorite book about money is Brent Kessler's *It's Not About The Money*. Kessler says he is a financial planner by day and a yogi by dawn. It was his yoga and meditation practice of decades that helped him learn how to truly help others financially. Why? Because he got in touch with the concept of the *"wanting mind."* We all have it. It comes from our biological need for survival, and it is always wanting. It is always craving an experience different from the one it currently has. The *wanting mind* is always future focused, never paying attention to what is. It insists that things need to change in order to be happy. And the wanting mind doesn't care if you have millions of dollars or not enough dollars. It still wants. And it is, by its very nature, addictive. **The more it wants, the more it wants.** If your *wanting mind* is in control, you will never learn to live within your means. We must learn not to take the *wanting mind* personally. We must learn to understand it for what it is: an often-powerful temporary state of mind that is likely to dissipate if we do not indulge it. It is not usually our hearts' truest desires or our deepest values.

Because many of us don't learn to tame the *wanting mind*, and we don't learn the difference between the *wanting mind* and our hearts' truest desires, many of us get in trouble with debt. Being over your head in debt can be a devastating way to live, and so many people are struggling to climb their way out of a hole of debt. Many twenty-somethings are swimming in student debt without a commensurate salary to match. Others have thousands of dollars in credit-card debt and have no idea what they actually purchased with all those thousands of dollars. A little here. A little there. How did I get in this mess? And then comes the avoidance of the problem. It seems so big, so overwhelming, so unmanageable, that it is easier to just stick our heads in the sand and pretend that we are not in trouble. **As with any thing you avoid, it just comes back at you harder and faster.**

Kessler makes a key point. You and I can never change our financial situation by changing our external circumstances. First, we have to change our inner world. We have to get in touch with our wanting mind, with our deepest desires, with our habitual ways of interacting with money, with core beliefs about money, and erroneous beliefs about money. If you are having trouble living within your means, I suggest the book and this inner work to you.

We all have a relationship with money. And like any relationship, it requires attention, focus, tune-ups, and understanding. Don't let your *wanting mind* get the best of you. Adulting is messy enough, so learn to live within your means, be wise about money, and pay attention to what is already marvelous.

LAUNCH Questions for Reflection and Discussion

What was the culture of money in your family? How did your family talk about money? Or not?

Have you ever tracked your expenses over the course of 90 days? What would it be like to do this and get a realistic picture of where your money goes? Could you do it with a partner?

What are your financial goals? For example, be out of debt by a certain time? Have a set amount of money in your savings account? Have you ever successfully saved for some big purchase?

What do you know about your wanting mind? How do you tame it?

LAUNCH Checklist

- ☐ Journal Tip: For one month, keep a money journal in which you write down every penny that you spend. Be honest. At the end of the month, add up your expenditures and put them in categories. Get a good look at your spending habits. There are Apps for this: "Mint" and "Spending Tracker" can help.

- ☐ Save 10% of whatever you bring home for 90 days.

- ☐ Give away 10% of whatever you bring home for 90 days.

- ☐ With each time you run your credit or debit card, ask yourself: "Is this a need or a want?" Just try it as a way of staying mindful about your money.

LAUNCH Resources

It's Not About The Money, by Brent Kessler

How To Manage Your Money: www.nerdwallet.com

Financial Peace, by Dave Ramsey. www.daveramsey.com

Simple Banking: www.simple.com

Everything in moderation, including moderation.

—Bill Sander

Invest in Your Health

by *Amy*

On a return trip to Furman University recently, I was intrigued with the changes in the dining hall. When I attended, we had ... maybe ... two choices of main meals. And some days, if we were lucky, there was a salad bar. On this day I saw about five "stations," kiosk-like places where you could get pasta, or pizza, or a sub, or salad, or juices, or a hot meal, like chicken pot pie. There was also a soft-serve ice-cream station, and a coffee bar. Choices, choices, choices. I was a little jealous. Then I reminded myself that choice is often overrated. It would be so easy to eat the less healthy things more often than the healthy things. Just like with Uber-delivery, Shippt, and fast food of every variety, we can order whatever we want to eat any time of the day or night. So many choices to manage. Good? Bad? Who knows?

Just like it is never too early to develop the good habits of managing your money, it is certainly never too early to begin investing in your health, to developing healthy habits. I remember being in college and enjoying the ready access to safe running and walking trails, a good pool, intramural fields, and dance classes. It was convenient. And that specific kind of convenience may change when you launch into the adult world.

Eat Well

Can you find ways to healthfully feed yourself? At a recent church retreat, I asked a few soon-to-be college graduates about these important skills. One of them said that when she started her first job, the first new habit she established was packing her own lunch. I asked her why this was important to her. She was clear that she could not only feed herself better by packing a healthy lunch, but that she was saving more than $50 per week by not eating lunch out. You do the math. That's $200 per month she is *not* spending eating out. Once you figure in the cost of her groceries, she's probably saving $150 or so per month—$1800 per year. Not too shabby for establishing a relatively easy, new habit. And, as you might have already intuited, investing in your health may actually help your money management!

The state of your health is both cumulative and random. You may not feel the effects of the way you mistreat your body in your twenties, but you will soon enough. And of course, you could be a model of a healthy life, and you could still get some random, devastating illness. So, you don't invest in your health as a promise of some measure of control or positive outcome. You invest in your health because it's best to do what you can do. You know the Serenity prayer, right? *"God grant me the serenity to accept the things I cannot change, the courage to change the things I can, and the wisdom to know the difference."* Written by Protestant theologian Reinhold Niebuhr, this oft-cited prayer reminds us to use the power we have to change the things we can.

One of my neighbors has been an organic vegan since before most people knew what that meant. It may have been 30 years or so ago when I had to have her explain veganism to me. She was the epitome of health. And then she got Stage 4 colon cancer. It was bad. After treatments she could barely walk down her driveway. She wasn't sure she was going to live. The doctors weren't very hopeful. And I would see her trying to walk the block and I would think, "She's not going to live." That was probably ten years ago. The last time I spoke with her, she said that while the cancer was pure hell, the doctors have told her that they are pretty convinced that it was her overall healthy body that saved her. That cumulative healthy life-style did matter, even if at first she wondered why she bothered. This is not an endorsement of veganism. It is just to say that a healthy body is more resilient and fortified if and when there is a health crisis.

Move

Enough about food. **We all need ways to keep moving!** I have heard it said lately that sitting is the new smoking. This scares the crap out of me because I sit for a living—maybe 6–8 hours a day and sometimes more. So, I have to be very conscious of moving. Most days I get in a walk, a workout, or a dance lesson. I chose an upstairs office so I would have to do the stairs every hour. I try and walk—at least around the block—during my lunch break. Occasionally I get on the floor in between clients and stretch or do a few yoga poses. What are the most enjoyable ways for you to move? Walk or ride a bike. Dance—salsa, tango, swing, square, boogie, free-style—it's all good. Swim. Practice yoga or Pilates. Run up and down the stairs at work or home. Park as far away from the door as possible. Garden. Take a walk. Play with a toddler.

De-stress

Launching into the adult world with all of its new demands is stressful. **So have ways of de-stressing.** Take extended breaks from technology, including television. Try just one night a week. Or maybe a few hours each day. Practice meditation or contemplative forms of prayer. Do something creative—paint, sing, play an instrument, sew, cook, garden, write, make something. Take long, soaking baths. Be creative with a group. Join a local or community band or choir. Look for a writing group or a class of some kind to take. Local universities, libraries, even stores often host events like this.

Rest

Learn how to rest deeply. This is the adulting skill I probably needed to learn the most. (And still---I am not a very good rester!) By resting I don't mean numbing out binge-watching your newest Netflix obsession, although some television watching isn't a bad thing. Resting is about re-connecting with the deepest part of you. It is about allowing time for the events of your life to integrate inside of you. It has to do with letting go of the "to-dos, shoulds, and ought-tos" and just being with yourself for a while. Generally it is completely unproductive. In my Christian faith, we talk about Sabbath. Sabbath means to stop doing. It is designed to remind us that the world will keep spinning if we stop working, achieving, producing, trying. It is, in effect, a faithful act that says we believe we are enough and we don't need to do anything else to be worthy and valuable. Sabbath allows us to listen to our deepest Selves.

A Little = A Lot

To be wholly healthy, paying attention to your physical, psychological, and spiritual health are all necessary for a good launch into the adult world. If you can imagine a triple helix— body, mind, spirit—then you can visualize how all of this is related. Everything you do to better yourself in one area will connect with and improve the other areas. Actually, investing in your health is a life-long skill. A little each day and you will develop those healthy habits that will be in your best interest and in the best interest of those whose lives are closely linked with yours. Investing in your health will make your messy world a little more marvelous, for sure.

LAUNCH Questions for Reflection and Discussion

How do you show that you value or de-value your health? When are you most likely to brush your health off and just hope for the best?

In what ways are you proactive regarding your health? What, if anything, are you ready to do more of that would be positive and healthy?

It is easy to take your health for granted in the decade of your 20s and 30s. What habits for life are you, or you would like to begin, establishing now that you hope will safeguard your health?

Are there group activities that would help you invest more in your own health?

Notes:

LAUNCH Checklist

☐ Journal Tip: A few times a week, just check in mindfully with your body and write down what you notice. What areas of your body are feeling good? Tight? Uncomfortable? Are you hungry? Tired? Lonely? Just do a mindfulness check and write down what you find.

☐ Take an assessment for whole-life health. Here's one: https://wheel oflife.noomii.com/

☐ Hold yourself accountable by keeping track of in writing your goals and your progress.

LAUNCH Resources

▪ Living Compass, a not-for-profit organization, helps you look at four major areas of your life: heart, mind, soul, and strength. There is a free assessment you can take and also many resources and training available. www.livingcompass.org

▪ There are more Apps than we can name. Pick one for you and use it. Better yet, use it with a friend!

▪ Same thing with books. There are more than we can name. Ask a friend. Google. Pick one and engage with your whole self.

There is no end to education. It is not that you read a book, pass an examination, and finish with education. The whole of life, from the moment you are born to the moment you die, is a process of learning.

—Jiddu Krishnamurti, Indian philosopher, speaker, and writer

Be a Life-Long Learner

by *Rhea*

Well, here we are at the end of a short book on how to get better at adulting. Have you learned anything in this process? We hope so because we both are dedicated to being life-long learners. Not only do our professions require continuing education, but it keeps us young, flexible, passionate, interested, and interesting. I love being a psychologist, if for no other reason than I have opportunities to learn every day, both in formal and informal ways.

I usually return from a professional conference with a "post-conference high." Just listening to a few days' worth of materials sparks my passion for knowledge. It doesn't seem to matter if it is new material or if I am listening to something with which I am already familiar, my mind will work to reorganize ideas, view some things with a new perspective, and formulate creative ideas. For those times when I am the one presenting at a conference, I am required to do research, learn new concepts, figure out the best ways to communicate with colleagues, and work to understand old material in new ways. I love it and yes, I am that nerd.

The more that you read, the more things you will know. The more that you learn, the more places you'll go. —Dr. Seuss

Teaching is another way that I am continually learning. When faced with a room of twenty very bright Honor's college students, or 70 fairly interested psychology majors, or 140 easily bored students looking for a relevant elective, I have to be on my game. Every semester, I try to know a little more based on the questions I'm asked in class. I can never know it all but I stay engaged in learning. It seems like the right thing to do when I'm asking my students to also be engaged in learning.

Not everyone is afforded this "culture of learning" through their jobs, but we all can find opportunities to expand and deepen our knowledge. Learning best occurs when we follow our own interests and curiosity. It might be an interest in learning to knit. It might be curiosity about World War II. It might be the desire to learn to play an instrument. It might be the need for a DIY project that you can't afford to pay someone else to do and that you KNOW you could do yourself if you just studied it a bit. You know this one, when something is out of your price range and you say to yourself, "I could do that!"

I once heard about a woman who picked a topic every year on her birthday and sought to learn as much as she could for a year. What a great idea.

Create a passion for learning, thus always growing. —Messy Marvelous

There is also a good reason for doing this. In 1986, Dr. David Snowden began a program of research at the University of Minnesota involving the School Sisters of Notre Dame. They were a group of nuns who lived extraordinarily long lives—most of them well into their late 90's. Commonly referred to as "The Nun Study," the researchers focused on aging in a population of women who were fairly alike and led lives that did not involve common risks in women's health: childbirth, intimate partner violence, smoking, substance use, etc. Additionally, most of the nuns were teachers and many had their Masters' degrees.

Snowden and his team looked at four things: 1) measures of physical health; 2) measures of mental health; 3) early journal writings (required for entry in to the convent and then encouraged throughout their lives); and, beginning in 1990, 4) their brains (donated after death) for pathology tests—taking slices and examining them microscopically. There were two primary discoveries. First, in their writings, the nuns who had particularly rich, descriptive writings from an early age showed fewer outward signs of aging (memory problems, verbal production, and other symptoms of Alzheimer's disease). Second, the pathology reports found that many nuns with signs of advanced Alzheimer's showed few cognitive or behavioral symptoms.

The researchers were curious about how this could be and combed through records of their interviews with the Sisters and realized that all of the women had been life-long learners. Not only were they teachers, but they worked well into their eighties; and after this late retirement, they took up learning something new to keep themselves engaged. Math teachers took up sewing, writing teachers took up music, music teachers began to garden. In other words, they learned something entirely new. And their brains grew new connections and expanded their networks of dendritic connections. And their quality of life (cognitive health) was easily maintained—despite having late-stage Alzheimer's.

Fascinating.

As a teacher of psychology, I have to add a little lesson that "correlation does not imply causation." Because of the design of the study, we cannot say that learning is the reason that the nuns had no symptoms of the Alzheimer's that was evident in their brains, but it is an intriguing finding and keeps researchers chasing down this interesting connection of lifestyle and disease expression.

Fascinating nonetheless.

It is also arguable that continued learning keeps us engaged and interesting. Engaged learning positions us to meet other engaged and interesting people. Just like our brains grow new connections, so do our social lives. Who knows what might happen when we get to know interesting people?

Endlessly fascinating.

Our lives are undoubtedly messier than the nuns of the School Sisters of Notre Dame, but we improve our chances of having a more marvelous life when we continue to learn.

LAUNCH Questions for Reflection and Discussion

In what ways—physically, mentally, psychologically, and spiritually—are you willing to challenge yourself?

Is your style more to approach or avoid when it comes to learning something new? If your response to this is "It depends!", break that down.

What is your history of learning? Did you learn easily or was learning a struggle? How do you prefer to learn now?

Notes:

LAUNCH Checklist

☐ Journal Tip: Make a list of 10 things you want to learn more about. Maybe pick one or two for this year and dive in!

☐ Take a class. Online, on YouTube, etc., or in person.

☐ Read. Let us repeat. Read (or listen, of course).

☐ Practice, practice, practice what you are learning. Mastery takes practice.

LAUNCH Resources

Consult your local colleges and universities for adult learning opportunities. These do not require degree-seeking status to enroll.

You can learn almost anything on YouTube. Go search and see!

The same is true in your local library—many resources are available in an online format. If not, your investment to learn about a new topic is still almost nothing. Many large library systems also offer classes and groups about particular topics.

Wrap-up and ProTips for Adulting

by Amy & Rhea

Here we are. We wrote this manuscript in the fall of 2019, before the outbreak of COVID-19 in the early months of 2020. Little did we know that people were going to need all the help they could get by the time this book went to press. (That includes US, too, as we ALL adapt to these weird, changing times.) Although we were in the editing process during the stay-at-home time, we have specifically not mentioned the virus as we hope that these skills will have more longevity than the current pandemic (fingers crossed!). We sincerely hope that when this arrives in your hands that you are safe and healthy and that there is an effective vaccine available.

Adulting is an on-going, life-long journey. We are all forever growing, changing, evolving, and transforming. You are well on your way to adulting, and so you might be wondering where to go next. If you want to keep working on your adulting skills, here are some more ideas for you.

LAUNCH ProTips

Wash your hands.

Wear a mask (as long as needed to stop the spread of the virus).

Be kind.

Make your bed.

Read. A lot. Read things that challenge you.

Share.

Call your grandmother (or grandfather or aunt—anyone who has helped you along the way).

Rest.

Eat well.

Move.

Get outside as much as possible, even if for only a few minutes.

Admit when you're wrong.

Clean up after yourself.

Notice what needs to be done and do it.

Do your best at your job.

Look for solutions.

Believe in something bigger than you.

Support local businesses.

Look out for the little guy.

Be a global citizen.

Reuse, recycle, reduce.

Take care of those you love.

If there are skills you want to know more about, write us at DearLife@MessyMarvelous.com

About the Authors

Dr. Amy Sander Montanez has been in private practice since 1988. She holds a Master's Degree in Counseling from Clemson University and a D.Min. in Spiritual Formation from Graduate Theological Institute. In 2013, Amy's first book, *Moment to Moment: The Transformative Power of Everyday Life,* was awarded Spirituality and Health's Top 100 books of the year. Amy works  with all aspects of women's issues, emerging adults, couples and families, and grief. She is known for her work with clergy of all denominations and seminarians. Outside of the office she loves to cook and entertain, play the piano, listen to live music, ballroom dance, read, and gather with friends and family. Her husband, Nick, and daughter, Maria, are huge sources of joy in her life. www.amysandermontanez.com

Dr. Rhea Ann Merck has worked in the field of mental health since 1984. She earned her M.S. and Ph.D. in Psychology from the University of North Texas in Counseling Psychology and has maintained a private practice in Columbia, SC, since 1996. Rhea has worked in a variety of clinical settings with adults, emerging adults, teens, couples, and families. She currently  teaches Psychology at the University of South Carolina where she also consults with the Athletic Department. In 2019–2020, she was honored with the UofSC College of Arts and Sciences Undergraduate Teaching Award. In her free time, Rhea enjoys live music, yoga, painting, writing, entertaining, travel, and anything that brings her together with friends and family.

Notes:

Notes:

Notes:

Made in the USA
Monee, IL
16 April 2021